D1436111

YOU
ARE
MY
SUNSHINE

summersdale

YOU ARE MY SUNSHINE

An Hachette UK Company
www.hachette.co.uk

Summersdale Publishers Ltd
Part of Octopus Publishing Group Limited
Carmelite House
50 Victoria Embankment
LONDON
EC4Y 0DZ
UK

www.summersdale.com

Printed and bound in China

ISBN: 9-781-78783-541-2

Substantial discounts on bulk quantities of Summersdale books
are available to corporations, professional associations and other
organizations. For details contact general enquiries: telephone:
+44 (0) 1243 771107 or email: enquiries@summersdale.com.

To My dearest and special friend yvonne

ots of lo From nicola

x x x

Friendship's the wine of life.

EDWARD YOUNG

SHARED JOY IS A DOUBLE
JOY; SHARED SORROW
IS HALF A SORROW.

SWEDISH PROVERB

YOU

MAKE

THE GREYEST

OF DAYS

BRIGHTER

A FRIEND
IS SOMEONE
WHO KNOWS ALL
ABOUT YOU
AND STILL
LOVES YOU.

ELBERT HUBBARD

EACH FRIEND REPRESENTS A
WORLD IN US, A WORLD POSSIBLY
NOT BORN UNTIL THEY ARRIVE.

ANAÏS NIN

FRIENDSHIP...
FLOURISHES NOT SO
MUCH BY KINDNESSES
AS BY SINCERITY.

ÉTIENNE DE LA BOÉTIE

I ALWAYS FELT THAT THE
GREAT HIGH PRIVILEGE,
RELIEF AND COMFORT OF
FRIENDSHIP WAS THAT ONE
HAD TO EXPLAIN NOTHING.

KATHERINE MANSFIELD

"Stay" is a charming
word in a friend's
vocabulary.

AMOS BRONSON ALCOTT

A GOOD FRIEND IS...
A TIE TO THE PAST,
A ROAD TO THE FUTURE,
THE KEY TO SANITY.

LOIS WYSE

Thank you
for being you,
and accepting
me as I am

Friends are
true twins
in soul.

WILLIAM PENN

AGAINST THE
ASSAULT OF LAUGHTER,
NOTHING CAN STAND.

MARK TWAIN

FROM THE SPIRIT'S
CHOICE AND FREE DESIRE,
NEEDING NO OATH OR
LEGAL BOND, IS FRIEND
BESTOWED ON FRIEND.

DIETRICH BONHOEFFER

YOU
GIVE ME
REASONS
TO SMILE

THOSE WHO BRING
SUNSHINE INTO THE
LIVES OF OTHERS
CANNOT KEEP IT
FROM THEMSELVES.

J. M. BARRIE

MANY PEOPLE WILL
WALK IN AND OUT OF
YOUR LIFE, BUT ONLY
TRUE FRIENDS WILL
LEAVE FOOTPRINTS
IN YOUR HEART.

ELEANOR ROOSEVELT

You reassure
me when I need
it the most

Ah, how good it feels!
The hand of an old friend.

HENRY WADSWORTH LONGFELLOW

NEVER ABOVE YOU.
NEVER BELOW YOU.
ALWAYS BESIDE YOU.

WALTER WINCHELL

A day without laughter is a day wasted.

NICOLAS CHAMFORT

You push me
to be the very
best I can be

True friendship
is like sound health;
the value of it is seldom
known until it be lost.

CHARLES CALEB COLTON

I cherish everything about you

YOU
LIFT ME UP
WHEN I'M
DOWN

66

FRIENDS ARE THE
SUNSHINE OF LIFE.

JOHN HAY

99

A REAL FRIEND
IS ONE WHO WALKS
IN WHEN THE REST
OF THE WORLD
WALKS OUT.

WALTER WINCHELL

SOME PEOPLE
GO TO PRIESTS;
OTHERS TO POETRY;
I TO MY FRIENDS.

VIRGINIA WOOLF

You know
me better
than I
know myself

WHEN WE GIVE CHEERFULLY
AND ACCEPT GRATEFULLY,
EVERYONE IS BLESSED.

MAYA ANGELOU

I am wealthy in my friends.

WILLIAM SHAKESPEARE

Friendship is the greatest therapy

THE BETTER PART OF
ONE'S LIFE CONSISTS
OF HIS FRIENDSHIPS.

ABRAHAM LINCOLN

A friend is one of
the nicest things you
can have, and one of the
best things you can be.

DOUGLAS PAGELS

I WILL FOLLOW YOU
TO THE ENDS OF THE WORLD.

KHALED HOSSEINI

YOU
CONSTANTLY
PUSH ME
TO BE
MYSELF

A FRIEND IS
SOMEONE WHOSE
FACE YOU CAN SEE
IN THE DARK.

FRANCES O'ROARK DOWELL

You always
have my best
interests at heart

Friends like you do not come along often

AN UNSHARED HAPPINESS
IS NOT HAPPINESS.

BORIS PASTERNAK

One joy
scatters a
hundred
griefs.

CHINESE PROVERB

TRUE FRIENDS ARE
ALWAYS TOGETHER
IN SPIRIT.

L. M. MONTGOMERY

You believe in me
even when I don't
believe in myself

For a friend with an
understanding heart is worth
no less than a brother.

HOMER

IF YOU HAVE NOTHING
IN LIFE BUT A GOOD
FRIEND, YOU'RE RICH.

MICHELLE KWAN

YOU'RE
ALWAYS
HONEST

WHEREVER YOU
GO, NO MATTER
WHAT THE WEATHER,
ALWAYS BRING YOUR
OWN SUNSHINE.

ANTHONY J. D'ANGELO

Thank you
for all that you've
taught me

NO MAN IS USELESS
WHILE HE HAS A FRIEND.

ROBERT LOUIS STEVENSON

I'm lucky
to have
a friend
like you

I CAN TRUST MY FRIENDS.
THESE PEOPLE FORCE ME
TO EXAMINE MYSELF,
ENCOURAGE ME TO GROW.

CHER

THERE IS NO INVESTMENT
YOU CAN MAKE WHICH
WILL PAY YOU SO WELL
AS THE EFFORT TO
SCATTER SUNSHINE
AND GOOD CHEER.

ORISON SWETT MARDEN

Laughter
is a sunbeam
of the soul.

THOMAS MANN

They may forget what
you said – but they will
never forget how you
made them feel.

CARL W. BUEHNER

IN THE SWEETNESS OF FRIENDSHIP
LET THERE BE LAUGHTER...
FOR IN THE DEW OF LITTLE THINGS
THE HEART... IS REFRESHED.

KAHLIL GIBRAN

FRIENDSHIP NEEDS
NO WORDS – IT IS
SOLITUDE DELIVERED
FROM THE ANGUISH
OF LONELINESS.

DAG HAMMARSKJÖLD

YOU ALWAYS KNOW HOW TO CHEER ME UP

*A good laugh
is sunshine in
the house.*

WILLIAM MAKEPEACE THACKERAY

A TRUE FRIEND IS ONE
WHO OVERLOOKS YOUR
FAILURES AND TOLERATES
YOUR SUCCESS!

DOUG LARSON

You
inspire me
every day

I KEEP MY FRIENDS
AS MISERS DO THEIR
TREASURE, BECAUSE, OF
ALL THE THINGS GRANTED
US BY WISDOM, NONE
IS GREATER OR BETTER
THAN FRIENDSHIP.

PIETRO ARETINO

A FRIEND IS SOMEONE
WHO GIVES YOU TOTAL
FREEDOM TO BE YOURSELF —
AND ESPECIALLY TO FEEL,
OR NOT FEEL.

JIM MORRISON

Let us learn to show
our friendship for a man
when he is alive and
not after he is dead.

F. SCOTT FITZGERALD

THE FRIEND WHO
HOLDS YOUR HAND
AND SAYS THE WRONG
THING IS MADE OF
DEARER STUFF THAN
THE ONE WHO
STAYS AWAY.

BARBARA KINGSOLVER

FRIENDS ARE LIKE MELONS.
SHALL I TELL YOU WHY?
TO FIND ONE GOOD, YOU
MUST A HUNDRED TRY.

CLAUDE MERMET

FEW DELIGHTS
CAN EQUAL THE
MERE PRESENCE OF
ONE WHOM WE
TRUST UTTERLY.

GEORGE MACDONALD

YOU'RE THERE EVEN WHEN WE ARE MILES APART

FRIENDS ARE
THOSE RARE PEOPLE
WHO ASK HOW WE ARE
AND THEN WAIT TO
HEAR THE ANSWER.

ED CUNNINGHAM

BUT I HAVE MADE HIM
MY FRIEND, AND NOW HE IS
UNIQUE IN ALL THE WORLD.

ANTOINE DE SAINT-EXUPÉRY

A **DAY** SPENT
WITH **YOU**
IS A DAY
WELL SPENT

Friendship isn't a big thing –
it's a million little things.

ANONYMOUS

WHEN IT COMES TO
FRIENDS, IT'S NOT
HOW MUCH TIME YOU
SPEND WITH THEM, JUST
HOW YOU SPEND IT!

EIICHIRO ODA

You make me laugh
even when I don't
want to smile

You have
a heart
of gold

WHAT DO YOU MOST
VALUE IN YOUR FRIENDS?
THEIR CONTINUED EXISTENCE.

CHRISTOPHER HITCHENS

YOU
HELP ME
TO SEE MY
STRENGTHS

THE ORNAMENT OF
A HOUSE IS THE FRIENDS
WHO FREQUENT IT.

RALPH WALDO EMERSON

TO LOVE, AND TO
BE LOVED, IS THE
GREATEST HAPPINESS
OF EXISTENCE.

SYDNEY SMITH

CARE ABOUT
THE BEINGS YOU
CARE ABOUT IN
GORGEOUS AND
SURPRISING WAYS.

ANNE HERBERT

YOU
TAKE PRIDE
IN MY
ACHIEVEMENTS

I know
that I can
always turn
to you

WE MUST EVER
BE FRIENDS; AND OF
ALL WHO OFFER YOU
FRIENDSHIP LET ME BE
EVER THE FIRST, THE
TRUEST, THE NEAREST
AND DEAREST!

HENRY WADSWORTH LONGFELLOW

A true friend never
gets in your way unless
you happen to be
going down.

ARNOLD H. GLASOW

TOO OFTEN WE
UNDERESTIMATE THE
POWER OF A TOUCH, A
SMILE, A KIND WORD,
A LISTENING EAR... ALL
OF WHICH HAVE THE
POTENTIAL TO TURN
A LIFE AROUND.

LEO BUSCAGLIA

You're the light
at the end of
the tunnel

I GOT YOU TO
LOOK AFTER ME,
AND YOU GOT ME
TO LOOK AFTER YOU,
AND THAT'S WHY.

JOHN STEINBECK

IF I AM
NOT TOUCHING
A LIFE, I AM NOT
TOUCHING LIFE.

CRAIG D. LOUNSBROUGH

YOU GIVE THE BEST ADVICE

SOMETIMES PEOPLE ARE
BEAUTIFUL. NOT IN LOOKS.
NOT IN WHAT THEY SAY.
JUST IN WHAT THEY ARE.

MARKUS ZUSAK

Fate chooses
our relatives,
we choose our
friends.

JACQUES DeLILLE

THE UNIVERSE
ONLY MAKES SENSE
WHEN WE HAVE
SOMEONE TO SHARE
OUR FEELINGS WITH.

PAULO COELHO

I can't be
angry when
you're around

Love is rarer than
genius itself. And friendship
is rarer than love.

CHARLES PÉGUY

I HAVE LOVED MY
FRIENDS AS I DO VIRTUE,
MY SOUL, MY GOD.

THOMAS BROWNE

You know how to
make me laugh
with just a look

A REAL FRIENDSHIP
SHOULD NOT FADE
AS TIME PASSES, AND
SHOULD NOT WEAKEN
BECAUSE OF SPACE
SEPARATION.

JOHN NEWTON

THERE IS NOTHING I
WOULD NOT DO FOR
THOSE WHO ARE REALLY
MY FRIENDS. I HAVE
NO NOTION OF LOVING
PEOPLE BY HALVES.

JANE AUSTEN

THE FINEST FRIENDSHIPS
ARE BETWEEN THOSE WHO
CAN DO WITHOUT EACH OTHER.

ELBERT HUBBARD

YOU
LISTEN
WHEN I
HAVE A
PROBLEM

A friend is a gift you give yourself.

ROBERT LOUIS STEVENSON

A GOOD COMPANION
SHORTENS THE
LONGEST ROAD.

TURKISH PROVERB

You make
life better by
just being a
part of it

The best way to cheer
yourself up is to try to
cheer somebody else up.

MARK TWAIN

NO LOVE, NO FRIENDSHIP
CAN CROSS THE PATH OF OUR
DESTINY WITHOUT LEAVING
SOME MARK ON IT FOREVER.

FRANÇOIS MAURIAC

THERE'S NOTHING
WORTH THE WEAR
OF WINNING, BUT
LAUGHTER AND THE
LOVE OF FRIENDS.

HILAIRE BELLOC

You take away
sadness and replace
it with happiness

FRIENDSHIP IS THE
ONLY CURE FOR
HATRED, THE ONLY
GUARANTEE OF PEACE.

BUDDHA

IF I HAD A SINGLE
FLOWER FOR EVERY TIME
I THINK ABOUT YOU,
I COULD WALK FOREVER
IN MY GARDEN.

CLAUDIA ADRIENNE GRANDI

YOU
ALWAYS
ENCOURAGE
ME to
TRYING

Friendship is a
sheltering tree.

SAMUEL TAYLOR COLERIDGE

WORDS ARE EASY,
LIKE THE WIND;
FAITHFUL FRIENDS
ARE HARD TO FIND.

RICHARD BARNFIELD

Some friendships are made by nature, some by contract, some by interest, and some by souls.

JEREMY TAYLOR

You always
lift my
spirits

I WOULD RATHER WALK
WITH A FRIEND IN THE DARK,
THAN ALONE IN THE LIGHT.

HELEN KELLER

I FEEL THAT THERE
IS NOTHING MORE
TRULY ARTISTIC THAN
TO LOVE PEOPLE.

VINCENT VAN GOGH

You never
fail to brighten
my day

OUR TRIUMPHS
SEEM HOLLOW UNLESS
WE HAVE FRIENDS TO
SHARE THEM, AND OUR
FAILURES ARE MADE
BEARABLE BY THEIR
UNDERSTANDING.

JAMES RACHELS

THE GREATEST GIFT
OF LIFE IS FRIENDSHIP, AND
I HAVE RECEIVED IT.

HUBERT HUMPHREY

A true
friend is forever
a friend.

GEORGE MACDONALD

Friendship is always
a sweet responsibility,
never an opportunity.

KAHLIL GIBRAN

ALL WHO JOY
WOULD WIN
MUST SHARE IT.
HAPPINESS WAS
BORN A TWIN.

LORD BYRON

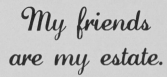

My friends
are my estate.

EMILY DICKINSON

You always
know the
right thing
to say

IF YOU HAVE ONE TRUE
FRIEND YOU HAVE MORE
THAN YOUR SHARE.

THOMAS FULLER

A SINGLE ROSE CAN
BE MY GARDEN;
A SINGLE FRIEND,
MY WORLD.

LEO BUSCAGLIA

SOMETIMES
THE MOST ORDINARY
THINGS COULD BE MADE
EXTRAORDINARY, SIMPLY
BY DOING THEM WITH
THE RIGHT PEOPLE.

NICHOLAS SPARKS

Thank you for being
a safe place for
me to turn to

A FRIEND IS WORTH ALL
HAZARDS WE CAN RUN.

EDWARD YOUNG

Friendship!
Mysterious
cement of
the soul.

ROBERT BLAIR

True happiness is...
the friendship and conversation
of a few select companions.

JOSEPH ADDISON

THERE IS NO EXERCISE
BETTER FOR THE HEART
THAN REACHING DOWN
AND LIFTING PEOPLE UP.

JOHN ANDREW HOLMES

Rare as
is true love,
true friendship
is rarer.

JEAN DE LA FONTAINE

THERE IS NOTHING BETTER
THAN A FRIEND, UNLESS IT IS A
FRIEND WITH CHOCOLATE.

LINDA GRAYSON

Your zest
for life is
contagious

YOU CAN'T DENY
LAUGHTER, WHEN
IT COMES; IT PLOPS
DOWN IN YOUR
FAVOURITE CHAIR
AND STAYS AS LONG
AS IT WANTS.

STEPHEN KING

LET US BE GRATEFUL TO
PEOPLE WHO MAKE US
HAPPY; THEY ARE THE
CHARMING GARDENERS
WHO MAKE OUR
SOULS BLOSSOM.

MARCEL PROUST

You remind me
that while there
is rain, there are
also rainbows

FOR YOU,
A THOUSAND
TIMES OVER.

KHALED HOSSEINI

Best friend,
my well-spring in
the wilderness!

GEORGE ELIOT

BUT FRIENDSHIP
IS PRECIOUS,
NOT ONLY IN
THE SHADE, BUT
IN THE SUNSHINE
OF LIFE.

THOMAS JEFFERSON

NOTHING
CHANGES
WHEN WE'VE
BEEN APART

The jewel in my dower, I would
not wish any companion
in the world but you.

WILLIAM SHAKESPEARE

NO ONE IS USELESS
IN THIS WORLD WHO
LIGHTENS THE BURDEN OF
IT TO ANYONE ELSE.

CHARLES DICKENS

I value your honesty and integrity

THERE IS ONE FRIEND
IN THE LIFE OF EACH
OF US WHO SEEMS
NOT A SEPARATE
PERSON, HOWEVER
DEAR AND BELOVED,
BUT AN EXPANSION,
AN INTERPRETATION,
OF ONE'S SELF.

EDITH WHARTON

A TRUE FRIEND
IS ONE WHO IS,
AS IT WERE, A
SECOND SELF.

CICERO

SINCE THERE IS NOTHING
SO WELL WORTH HAVING
AS FRIENDS, NEVER LOSE
A CHANCE TO MAKE THEM.

FRANCESCO GUICCIARDINI

A FRIEND IS A
PERSON WITH WHOM
I MAY BE SINCERE.
BEFORE HIM I MAY
THINK ALOUD.

RALPH WALDO EMERSON

*I felt it
shelter to speak
to you.*

EMILY DICKINSON

You're like
a shooting star
in a clear
night's sky

The best friend is he that,
when he wishes a person's
good, wishes it for that
person's own sake.

ARISTOTLE

YOU'RE THE
PERSON
I CAN
ALWAYS
RELY ON

A MAN'S FRIENDSHIPS
ARE ONE OF THE BEST
MEASURES OF HIS WORTH.

CHARLES DARWIN

WE HAVE EACH OF
US CAUSE TO THINK
WITH DEEP GRATITUDE
OF THOSE WHO HAVE
LIGHTED THE FLAME
WITHIN US.

ALBERT SCHWEITZER

FRIENDSHIP
IS THE GREATEST
OF WORLDLY GOODS.
CERTAINLY TO ME
IT IS THE CHIEF
HAPPINESS OF LIFE.

C. S. LEWIS

FRIENDSHIP, LIKE
PHOSPHORUS, SHINES
BRIGHTEST WHEN
ALL AROUND IS DARK.

PROVERB

You
are my
sunshine

If you're interested in finding out more about our books, find us on Facebook at Summersdale Publishers and follow us on Twitter at @Summersdale.

www.summersdale.com